D1005713

Dearest
Elizabeth,

STARS ABOARD

thought you would
little this —
greetings
from QM2

Designed and produced by

The Open Agency
Mill House
8 Mill Street
London SE1 2BA

Written by **Elspeth Wills**

First published 2003
© The Open Agency Limited
All images © Cunard Line

ISBN 0-9542451-2-1

Printed in China

STARS ABOARD

Celebrities of yesteryear who travelled Cunard Line
during the golden age of transatlantic travel.

INTRODUCTION

Cunarders have carried the rich and famous across the Atlantic since the Britannia set out on her maiden voyage in 1840 with founder Samuel Cunard on board.

Cunard's entry into the celebrity game however, was far from auspicious. On his way to read extracts from his novels to admiring audiences in the USA, the English author Charles Dickens travelled on the Britannia in 1842. He described his cabin as 'a preposterous box', the saloon as a 'gigantic hearse with windows' and the cook as 'secretly swigging damaged whiskey'. On arrival in Boston he vowed: 'if it pleases Heaven - never to cross the Ocean in a steamer again.'

He broke his promise in 1867 when he returned from another American tour on the Cunard steamship, the Russia. On this voyage he found things much more to his liking: 'the ship was fragrant with flowers.' and 'bubbles of champagne pervaded the nose.' By now Atlantic travel was newsworthy. The provincial press placed announcements that their town's most prominent citizens had 'left on the Cunard Steamship Line for Europe', while New York newspapers set up dedicated news desks to cover the movements of ships in port.

By the early 20th century millionaires, society hostesses, politicians and actresses were on the move on the new luxury liners. Intending travellers scoured passenger lists to check if their friends were on board or whom they should 'cut' in the dining room. Etiquette writers advised the nouveau riche on how to rub shoulders with the aristocracy and the titled on how to shake off the shipboard bore. Cunard briefed its captains as to whom to invite to their table and tipped off the press as to whether royalty was on board.

The arrival of a liner in New York Harbor attracted a swarm of reporters and photographers nicknamed 'Gangplank Willies'. In pursuit of a scoop the keenest newshounds hitched a ride on any boat scheduled to meet the liner as she came into port. According to one hard-bitten reporter: 'An ocean trip makes people want to talk.' Commodore Bisset, one of Cunard's most famous captains, confirmed this impression in the 1920s: 'Very few celebrities are shy of reporters. That is one reason why they are celebrities.'

Until the advent of commercial flight, a liner was the only way to cross. The likely presence of celebrities was part of the romance and excitement of the voyage. The cinema added a new dimension as aspiring British actors and actresses headed for Hollywood and established stars travelled to Europe to promote their latest picture.

Cunard looked after its celebrities impeccably. Dorothy Lamour refused to travel unless she could secure her favourite cabin on the promenade deck. On her honeymoon on the Mauretania film star Lana Turner ordered raw minced beef with raw eggs beaten into it for breakfast, washed down by champagne of course. The Queen Mother, who enjoyed an evening at the cinema, liked to be called just before the main feature to avoid the cartoons that preceded it.

Famous people on board attracted gossip and legendary tales. Helena Rubinstein is supposed to have tossed her 20 carat diamond earrings out of the porthole, forgetting that she had hidden them for safety in the tissue box that she was discarding. Cary Grant proposed to one of his five wives on the Queen Mary, while film producer Samuel Goldwyn stalked her decks with his camera at the ready in case he spotted a photogenic new face. Marlene Dietrich followed her friend Noel Coward's advice - 'always be seen, dear ... always be seen.' - by timing her entrance to the dining room for maximum effect. She was never seen at breakfast and only rarely at lunch.

On the Queen Mary the Duke of Windsor walked the dogs while the Duchess joined him in endless games of canasta after dinner. Ray Milland and his wife went shopping for tweed, Fred Astaire swept his partner round the ballroom and Bob Hope practised his golf swing on deck. Some celebrities used the five day voyage to escape the public eye. Notoriously publicity-shy Greta Garbo travelled incognito and disembarked disguised as a stewardess while Bing Crosby sought refuge in the darkroom where he chatted to the photographers as they developed that day's film.

The idea of onboard photography came to young Casimir Watkins over a cocktail with a Cunard director as the Berengaria steamed across the Atlantic. Borrowing £500 from an uncle, he set up the first Ocean Pictures studio on the Lancastria in 1929, later winning the exclusive right to onboard photography on the Queen Mary and the Queen Elizabeth. Staff were briefed to be discreet as they mingled with passengers: overstepping the mark led to instant dismissal. Photographers worked through the night to develop their film so that passengers could select the prints that they wished to order the next morning.

Most of the photographs in this book come from this unique visual record of life on board in the days when the great Atlantic liners carried the cream of international society. This is the first time that many of these images, which now form part of the Cunard archives, have been put on public view. Some photographs have details of when, where and why they were taken and who the subject was while others simply have a virtually illegible scrawl on the back. Some names are legendary and some faces unmistakeable - Sir Winston Churchill, Charles Chaplin or Ella Fitzgerald. Time has been less kind to other personalities famous in their day but now only recalled by a faded print of a pose beside a lifebelt or among the floral tributes of a first class stateroom.

This book celebrates the golden days of transatlantic travel and the remarkable individuals who chose the ultimate way to cross. It was the one time when stars could escape the limelight and ordinary passengers were treated like stars.

WHO'S WHO

EDDIE ARCARO
(1916-1997)

Which one was 'Banana Nose'?

Eddie Arcaro gained a number of nicknames in his lifetime including 'Banana Nose' and 'Master'. The Ohio taxi driver's son was one of only two jockeys to become five times winner of the Kentucky Derby, the fastest two minutes in sport.

Leaving school at fourteen to become an exercise boy, he won his first race in 1932. Despite fracturing his skull and puncturing a lung in a fall the next year, by 1940 he was the top earning jockey in the USA.

Only eleven thoroughbreds have achieved the ultimate honour of US racing, the Triple Crown, winning the Kentucky Derby and the Preakness and Belmont Stakes in the same year. Arcaro rode two of the winning horses, Whirlaway (1941) and Citation (1947).

He was not Citation's first rider, taking over the horse when its jockey disappeared during a hunting expedition. Arcaro donated half the winnings from his second Triple Crown to that jockey's widow. In 1955, the year before his last Triple Crown race, author William Faulkner described Arcaro as 'hunched like a fly or a cricket on the big withers.'

In his career Arcaro raced 24,092 times, had 4,779 wins and accumulated over $30m in purse money.

Right Arcaro (right) swapped his riding gloves for boxing gloves in this bout with Ron Clayton in the onboard gym.

PEARL BAILEY
(1918-1988)

Ambassador of Love

Singer and actress Pearl Bailey was the daughter of a Virginia preacher. Talent competitions were her route to success. Her victory in a singing contest in 1938 at the Apollo Theater in Harlem, New York's black entertainment quarter, led to singing with big bands.

From starring in the 1946 Broadway musical 'St Louis Woman', her career encompassed film, television, stage and cabaret including the all-black stage version of 'Hello Dolly' (1967) which won her a Tony, the top theatrical award. Bailey was known for her throaty, sexy voice and her mischievous, down-to-earth personality.

A deeply spiritual person, Pearl Bailey, known to the world as 'Pearlie Mae', became increasingly involved in humanitarian causes, President Nixon naming her America's 'Ambassador of Love'. Retiring from show business in 1975, she took a theology degree and devoted the rest of her life to campaigning for improved literacy and support for AIDS victims. She became a US Goodwill Ambassador to the United Nations.

Left Furs kept out the chill Atlantic breezes on the Queen Elizabeth.

CECIL BEATON
(1904-1980)

On the receiving end

Sir Cecil Beaton was one of the 20th century's greatest photographers. His upper class background gave him an entrée into the world of London society and 'bright young things'. He photographed debutantes and royalty and added his own elegant touch to the faces of film stars such as Katharine Hepburn, Greta Garbo and Audrey Hepburn. He memorably captured the tragic beauty of the shipping line heiress Nancy Cunard.

From the 1950s he turned his eye for glamour to costume design winning Academy Awards for 'Gigi' and 'My Fair Lady' (1964). He was so attuned to changes in fashion that his career maintained its momentum into the 1960s and beyond, photographing icons like the Rolling Stones, the ballet dancer Rudolph Nureyev and the model Twiggy.

Cecil Beaton was famous for his waspish humour. When the mini skirt made its first appearance in the 1960s, he commented: 'Never in the history of fashion has so little material been raised so high to reveal so much that needs to be covered so badly.'

Right Cecil Beaton keeping a weather eye open on the Queen Mary. He was one of the privileged passengers who joined her historic maiden voyage in 1936.

BELITA
(1923-)

Escapades on ice

The name Nether Wallop sounds like Hollywood's idea of an idyllic English village. In reality Belita, one of its most famous inhabitants, travelled on skates all the way from Nether Wallop to Tinseltown.

Belita was born Gladys Lyne Jepson-Turner. A skating star by the age of 14, she crossed the Atlantic and soon was the leading lady of the Ice-Capades who performed extravaganzas with numbers such as 'Polka Dots 'N' Dashes' and 'Winter Wonderland'. She also pursued a career as a professional skater, being placed seventh in the 1937 World Skating Championships.

'Ice-Capades' transferred to the screen in 1942 bringing Belita to the attention of film directors who spotted her acting potential. She added a touch of glamour to a series of film noirs with titles like 'Suspense' and 'The Gangster' and in the 1950s featured in several of Hollywood's greatest musicals. Her star year was 1957 when she joined Fred Astaire in 'Silk Stockings' and Gene Kelly in 'Invitation to the Dance'.

Belita's most unusual appearance was in 1946 when she was invited to solve the murder mystery 'The Living Death' as guest armchair detective on Ellery Queen's radio show.

Left Belita took to the teak boards of a Cunarder deck.

GEORGE BURNS & GRACE ALLEN
(1896-1996 & 1902-1964)

A partnership made in heaven

Comedian George Burns was often asked how to make a marriage work: 'I tell them the answer's easy - marry Gracie.'

George met Grace Allen in 1922 when they were both aspiring vaudevillians. Under a number of stage names from Eddie DeLight to Jed Jackson, George had been a singer from the age of seven when he formed the Pee Wee Quartet with friends from New York's Lower East Side. He took more than a professional interest in partnering Gracie, declaring his love with a $20 wedding ring in 1926. On stage and later on screen, radio and television, the couple made millions laugh with their antics as man and wife. George wrote the material and played the long-suffering straight man while dizzy Gracie won the laughs.

'For 40 years my act consisted of one joke, then she died.' After Gracie's death in 1964, George tried out other comic partners but in the end had to admit that there was only one Gracie. In 1975 he made a dramatic comeback, winning an Oscar for his portrayal of a cantankerous old comedian in the film version of Neil Simon's 'The Sunshine Boys'. Even when he reached his century, he remained as sharp witted as ever.

Right George Burns enjoyed the experience of sailing with Cunard, one of whose founders was also named George Burns. This was pure coincidence as the comedian was born Nathan Bimbaum.

HOAGY CARMICHAEL
(1899-1981)

Stardust over the ocean

The year 1899 witnessed three events that were to change the sound of American music forever. Scott Joplin published 'Maple Leaf Rag' and Duke Ellington, the maestro of jazz, and Hoagland Carmichael one of the first modern singer-songwriters, were born.

Hoagy's mother, who played the piano during 'silents' at the local cinema, taught him 'Maple Leaf Rag'. As a student he played ragtime while studying law, a profession he quickly abandoned for music. In 1927 he composed 'Star Dust', which, with added lyrics, became one of the most widely performed and recorded popular songs of all time.

In the 1930s he recorded with the bands of Jack Teagarden, Benny Goodman and Bix Biederbecke and penned jazz classics including 'Rockin' Chair' and 'Lazy River'. Moving to Hollywood in 1936 he turned his talents to musicals and film scores. He occasionally appeared in films himself usually in the guise of a pianist with a cigarette dangling from his lips.

Left Hoagy and his wife, Ruth Meinardi, on the Sports Deck of the Queen Elizabeth. On a previous wartime crossing he was one of the first to obey the command 'all hands on deck' when his ship hit a freak wave and damaged her bow.

Although now chiefly remembered as the composer of songs like 'My Resistance Is Low', 'Georgia' and 'In the Cool, Cool, Cool of the Evening', at the peak of his career in the 1940s Hoagy was singer, film and television actor, recording artiste, entertainer, radio and television performer, and author.

CHARLES CHAPLIN
(1889-1977)

The first ever film star

From early childhood Charlie Chaplin's goal was to be the most famous person in the world, although he spent much of it living on his wits on the streets of London. He cut his teeth in comedy through the rough and tumble of vaudeville and the circus.

In 1915 he made his first film appearance as the character that he was to make his own - the baggy suited Tramp with a moustache and a cane. By the early 1920s he was so successful that no studio could afford him and he had to make his own films. More tales of the Tramp followed including 'Gold Rush' (1925), the film he wanted to be remembered by.

Chaplin stood out against the 'talkies' until 1936 when in his classic 'Modern Times' the Tramp spoke for the first and only time. Increasingly he combined comedy with political comment, notably in the Great Dictator (1940). After the Second World War he fell foul of the McCarthy communist witch hunt and moved with Oona, the last of his five wives, to Switzerland where he continued to produce films until 1967. Only in 1972 was he invited back to the United States, to receive his second honorary Academy Award.

Right Charlie Chaplin and his wife Oona entertaining on the Queen Elizabeth.

WINSTON CHURCHILL

(1874-1965)

A debt of gratitude

At the end of the Second World War Sir Winston Churchill, British Prime Minister and world leader, summed up the role of the Queen Mary and the Queen Elizabeth in the Battle of the Atlantic.

'At a speed never before realised in war, they carried over a million men to defend the liberties of civilisation. Without their aid the day of final victory must unquestionably have been postponed. To the men who contributed to the success of our operations in the years of peril, and to those who brought these two great ships into existence, the world owes a debt of gratitude.'

Under the name of Colonel Warden, Churchill himself crossed the Atlantic four times on the Queen Mary, her speed and reliability being vital to his safe passage. In May 1943 he sailed to New York to meet President Roosevelt and set the date for the Allied invasion of Europe. Later that year he steamed to Halifax to attend the Quebec conference that planned the detail of D-day. In 1944 he made a two way crossing: although the tide of war was turning, he learned of the first V2 bomb attack on London while at sea.

Left Commodore Sir James Bisset letting Winston Churchill have a turn at the controls.

CLAUDETTE COLBERT
(1903-1996)

'The wickedest woman in history'

Claudette Colbert was one of Hollywood's greatest screwball
comediennes and the highest paid star of her day.

Her business head came from her father, a Paris banker who moved
his family to New York. As a student she forsook art for acting
although at first her looks and accent risked her being typecast as a
French maid. Her first major Hollywood success was as the wife of
the Roman Emperor Nero in Cecil B. deMille's Biblical epic 'Sign of
the Cross' (1932), followed two years later by the lead role in his
spectacular 'Cleopatra'. After most Hollywood actresses had turned
it down, she reluctantly took on the part of a spoilt runaway heiress
opposite Clark Gable in Frank Capra's 'It Happened One Night',
demanding twice her normal salary. The film swept the boards at
the 1935 Oscars.

A string of screwball comedies followed, interspersed with more
serious dramas such as the Orson Welles 1946 classic 'Tomorrow Is
Forever'. From the 1950s she forged a new career on stage and
television, spending much of her final years at her plantation house in
Barbados where Frank Sinatra and the Reagans were regular guests.

Right Wrapped in furs
to ward off the chill on
the Promenade Deck,
unusually Claudette
looked the camera
straight in the eye. She
had a phobia that only
her 'good side' was
to be photographed.

RONALD COLMAN
(1891-1958)

'The handsomest man on the screen'

Shy English public schoolboy Ronald Colman started out life as a shipping clerk.

When he took up acting in 1915, his striking looks and velvet voice soon got him noticed. In 1920 lack of work in Britain tempted him to try his luck in New York. After crossing the Atlantic with only £7 and a change of clothes to his name, he slowly picked up small stage and screen parts. He grew his famous moustache on the Atlantic en route to Italy to star in a romantic tear-jerker with Lillian Gish. The film made his name.

Colman transferred successfully to the talkies, his cultured British accent matching moviegoers' image of the dashing hero. His first talkie was 'Bulldog Drummond' (1929), a role which he made his own. In the 1930s he found time for a world cruise and to fall in love with his second wife. During the Second World War he entertained the troops and made two of his finest films. He won an Oscar for 'A Double Life' (1947) travelling with his wife on the Queen Elizabeth to attend its European premieres.

Appropriately for a former shipping clerk, Colman's last film appearance was a cameo role in 'Around the World in Eighty Days' (1956).

Left Ronald Colman and his British actress wife Benita Hume were regular Cunard passengers since 1938 when Benita cancelled her ticket home on the Queen Mary after he cabled her to marry him.

GARY COOPER
(1901-1961)

Hero on horseback

His past gives a clue as to how Gary Cooper managed to combine the rugged charm of the frontier with the poise of a gentleman. The son of a wealthy Montana lawyer, he went to school in England and perfected his riding skills back home on the ranch.

After failing as a newspaper cartoonist, 'Coop' found work as an extra in cowboy films. With practice his acting matched his looks and soon his laconic style of speech became the archetypal voice of the Western hero.

His first success was 'The Virginian' (1929) and his most notable performances were in the two Ernest Hemingway epics, 'A Farewell to Arms' (1932) and 'For Whom the Bell Tolls' (1943) and in 'High Noon' (1952). Although he will always be associated with the Western, his versatility led him to be cast as toff, adventurer, baseball star and war hero. He summed up the virtues of small town America in 'Mr Deeds Goes to Town' (1936) and 'Meet John Doe' (1941).

With 100 films and two Oscars under his belt, 'Coop' was honoured with a special Academy Award. His friend James Stewart accepted on his behalf inadvertently blurting out that Cooper had cancer. With Cooper's death within six months of Clark Gable, a chapter of Hollywood closed.

Right No need to worry about the lifebelts with 'Coop' on board. As a result of his punishing film schedule in the 1930s he was sent on a trip to Europe on doctor's orders.

LOU COSTELLO
(1908-1959)

'I'm a ba-a-ad boy'

Louis Francis Cristillo started his Hollywood career as a stuntman specialising in spectacular falls. While performing as a stage burlesque comedian in 1936 he approached another member of the cast to step in when his partner fell ill. The duo Abbott and Costello was born. Lou played the dumpy hapless fall-guy to Bud Abbott's taller, more serious, straight man.

They wrote their own routines, one of their most famous ones being 'Who's on First'. While crossing the Atlantic on the Queen Mary, they changed their baseball gags to football jokes to make their British audience laugh.

Radio, Broadway and Hollywood swiftly beckoned. With their second feature film 'Buck Privates' (1941) they were on their way to become Hollywood's biggest money-spinning duo.

Countless radio shows, two television series and 36 films later the partnership broke up in 1957.

Left It's Lou's turn to be on first.

SIR NOEL COWARD
(1899-1973)

'Why do the wrong people travel…

…and the right people stay at home.' The author of this lyric from 'Sail Away' was playwright, actor, cabaret performer and bon viveur, Noel Coward. He was the man who came to personify cocktails, caviar and Cunard.

In 1924 he starred in his own play 'The Vortex' which caused a sensation because of its treatment of drug abuse. Fifteen plays which captured the glamour of a generation swiftly followed including 'Hay Fever', 'Cavalcade' and 'Private Lives'.

During the Second World War Noel wrote moving film scripts including 'In Which We Serve' (1942) and 'Brief Encounter' (1946). When Twenties glamour went out of fashion he reinvented himself as a cabaret artist.

Noel Coward and Cunard went hand in hand. In 1921, when he had conquered London and was ready for Broadway, he bought a one-way ticket on the Aquitania. After paying for his ticket, a suitcase for his new wardrobe and a sheaf of scripts to sell to New York producers, he had exactly $85 left. He had to sell some songs to fund his trip.

He was one of the Queens' most frequent travellers winning over both passengers and crew with his repartee and social graces.

Right Noel Coward checking his luggage for his that elusive silk dressing gown.

BING CROSBY
(1904-1977)

'High society'

Harry Lillis Crosby is known to the world as Bing. As a child he called himself after his favourite cartoon strip 'The Bingville Bungle'.

His big break came in 1927 when the great band leader Paul Whiteman heard Bing's trio the Rhythm Boys and hired them. Bing's relaxed crooning of sentimental ballads helped to lift America out of the Depression blues. His carefully cultivated image of the happily married, regular guy chimed in with American values.

In 1932 he made the first of his 55 feature films 'The Big Broadcast'. His playing of C. K. Dexter Haven, the man who tamed Grace Kelly in 'High Society' (1956) was close to his own character - easy going, witty and charming.

Although from the 1950s he reduced his film commitments to allow more time on the golf course, no Christmas show was complete without Bing crooning 'White Christmas'.

His end was fitting. He collapsed shortly after playing the 18th hole on a Spanish golf course. In possibly the most successful musical career of all time he had recorded over 1,700 songs.

Left Bing was a regular on the Queen Mary. He made friends with the Ocean Pictures' photographers, often escaping to their darkroom for a chat.

MARLENE DIETRICH
(1901-1992)

The Devil is a Woman

After a year in the chorus line of a travelling revue, Marlene Dietrich trained as an actress in Berlin. Her break came in 1929 when she was spotted by American film director, Josef Von Sternberg, who cast her as Lola-Lola, the sultry nightclub vamp, in the German-American co-production 'The Blue Angel' (1930). They collaborated on a further six films including 'The Devil is a Woman' (1935). Von Sternberg aimed to make his protégée a second Greta Garbo.

Although the Nazis tried to lure her back to Germany with a lucrative film contract, Marlene Dietrich became an American citizen in 1939. She worked tirelessly for the war effort, entertaining troops, raising money and making anti-Nazi broadcasts in German. She was awarded the US Presidential Medal of Freedom and French Legion d'Honneur.

In the 1950s she launched a second career as a recording star and cabaret performer singing to packed houses throughout the world. She was a regular Cunard passenger, famous for never being seen at breakfast and rarely for lunch, and for her dramatic entrances at dinner. She followed the advice of her friend, the playwright Sir Noel Coward: 'Always be seen, darling, always be seen.'

Right Marlene Dietrich wrapped up against the chill Atlantic breezes on the Queen Elizabeth.

WALT DISNEY
(1901-1966)

Reserved for the Disneys

As well as film stars Cunarders carried the man who helped to create the Hollywood legend.

Being brought up on a farm introduced Walt Disney to some of the animals which later enthralled generations of children. During the First World War he camouflaged his Red Cross ambulance with cartoons. After working as a commercial artist, in 1923 he set up an animation studio in Hollywood. Mickey Mouse made his debut five years later in 'Steamboat Willie', the world's first fully-synchronised sound cartoon while 'Snow White and the Seven Dwarfs' (1937) was the first full-length musical cartoon.

From 1940 90% of the output of Disney's 1,000-strong team of artists, animators, writers and technicians was dedicated to war work. In the 1950s adventure films, wildlife features and television programmes rolled off the line. Whatever the new medium Disney embraced it.

During a 43-year career Walt Disney combined creativity, imagination, innovation and sound business sense to become a byword for entertainment. Disney and his team received more than 950 honours including 48 Oscars, his studio released hundreds of films and in 1955 he launched a new brand of entertainment, Disneyland, the most successful amusement park ever.

Left Walt Disney and family in the Dance Salon of the Queen Elizabeth, after a meal at the table they always reserved for its view of the Manhattan skyline in the sunset.

ADELE DIXON
(1908-1992)

First lady

2nd November 1936, was a remarkable day for musical comedy star Adele Dixon and for the British nation. It saw the launch of the first high resolution, public television service in the world.

Adele was the first entertainer to appear on the small screen, alongside American dancers Buck and Bubbles, and Chinese jugglers The Lai Founs. They were serenaded by the new BBC Television Orchestra. Fewer than 500 viewers witnessed this momentous occasion: to experience it they had to live within a 25 mile radius of the transmitter and own a set which cost about the same as a small car.

One of the numbers Adele sang was specially written for the occasion - 'Television'.

'A mighty maze of mystic, magic rays
Is all about us in the blue,
And in sight and sound they trace
Living pictures out of space
To bring a new wonder to you.'

The next year Adele achieved another first when the Broadway show in which she was appearing with Jack Buchanan and Evelyn Laye became the first American Command Performance, when presented to mark President F.D. Roosevelt's birthday.

When the BBC celebrated its 50th anniversary in 1986 Adele Dixon was traced to join the celebrations. The 78 year old never had a television set.

Right Adele Dixon making sure that her trunk stays shut even if the liner rolls.

PRESIDENT DWIGHT D. EISENHOWER
(1890-1969)

Ike's on board

In the early afternoon of June 5th, 1944 General Eisenhower came to a decision: 'OK, let's go'. Those few words from the Supreme Allied Commander launched the D-Day landings which proved to be the turning point of the Second World War.

Eisenhower masterminded the formation of the new North Atlantic Treaty Organisation in the year before he was persuaded to run for President in 1952. He won the election on the campaign slogan: 'I like Ike'.

He was a regular Cunard traveller. On 27th September, 1946, he arrived at Southampton with his wife Mamie on the Queen Mary at the end of her record breaking crossing of the Atlantic. Their son Captain John Eisenhower flew from Austria to meet them.

In April 1951 Eisenhower sailed to Europe on the Queen Elizabeth to continue his duties of setting up a 'United States of Europe' at the NATO headquarters in Paris.

Right General Eisenhower crossed the Atlantic several times on Cunarders during the Second World War and the setting up of NATO.

DUKE ELLINGTON
(1899-1974)

The Ellington effect

Duke Ellington was one of the greatest bandleaders and composers in the history of jazz. His childhood nickname, Duke, and his talent for playing the piano remained with him all his life.

In 1918 he formed his first group, the Duke's Serenaders, later taking over the Washingtonians which he expanded into a ten piece orchestra. On moving to the Cotton Club, the leading New York jazz venue, he created his legendary jungle sound of growling trumpets and trombones. Along with Louis Armstrong he dominated the 1930s jazz scene.

In 1943 Ellington launched a decade of annual concerts in Carnegie Hall with 'Black, Brown and Beige', a portrayal through sound of the history of African-Americans in the USA. From the 1950s he increasingly toured abroad. 'Take The A Train' was the orchestra's theme tune but when crossing the Atlantic Ellington travelled Cunard.

As a composer Ellington saw his orchestra as his instrument, writing over 2,000 pieces from popular songs to an unfinished opera and film scores. He knew the musical personalities of many of his players and wrote to draw out their talents. In a career that spanned four decades, he gave over 20,000 performances.

Left Duke Ellington calling up a storm on the boat deck of the Queen Elizabeth.

TOMMY FARR
(1914-1986)

'My face looked like a dug up road'

Welshman Tommy Farr took up boxing as the only way of escaping a lifetime down the local coal mine. Although he won his very first fight at the age of 12, 'The Tonypandy Terror' proved more of a loser than a winner until a string of twenty fights without defeat and the British and Empire Heavyweight Championship title put him firmly in the ring.

After an unexpected victory over former World Heavyweight Champion, Max Baer, Tommy was ready for the ultimate challenge, taking on one of the greatest World Heavyweight Champions of all time, Joe Louis in 1937. All the money was on the black American. Before a crowd of 32,000 in New York and with almost every radio set in Wales tuned in to the match, Tommy gave the 'Brown Bomber' the fight of his life. The 23 year old Welshman danced, crouched, bobbed, weaved and jabbed his way through 15 rounds before Joe Louis was declared the winner. Tommy's face had taken a battering but he had won the hearts of the world.

Left Tommy Farr in pugnacious pose beside one of the Queen Mary's lifebelts.

Although this was the highpoint of his career, Tommy continued to box until retirement in 1940 although near bankruptcy later forced him briefly back into the ring.

GRACIE FIELDS
(1898-1979)

Our Gracie

Gracie Fields was a much loved British institution. Born over her grandmother's fish and chip shop, her acting talent was encouraged by her mother who dreamed of going on the stage. Her career took off after meeting her comedy partner and future husband Archie Pitt and a nine year run of a revue made the couple wealthy.

In 1931 she appeared in the first of 16 films, 'Sally in our Alley' which gave rise to her signature tune 'Sally', a song that she grew to hate. Her sentimental songs, opera-class voice and broad Lancashire humour won her a place in the affections of the British public second only to the King and Queen, demonstrated when quarter of a million well-wishers wrote to her during a serious illness.

The fickle public turned against her during the Second World War because she chose to raise funds for the war effort in North America as her Italian second husband risked internment in Britain as an enemy alien. In her first major British appearance after the War she opened with 'Take Me to Your Heart Again'. Her audience gave her a standing ovation. Her final recognition came in 1978, a year after she sang 'Sally' for the last time, when the Queen Mother made her a Dame.

Right Two British institutions meet as Gracie Fields relaxes beside a mural of a harbour scene in the drawing room of the Queen Mary.

ELLA FITZGERALD
(1918-1996)

'The first lady of song'

When the 16 year old orphan came on stage at a Harlem Apollo Theater amateur night her intention was to dance but her nerve failed her. The compere told her to sing instead and she won first prize. She attracted the attention of New York bandleader Chick Webb who launched her on six decades of song. A swing version of the 1879 nursery rhyme 'A-Tisket A-Tasket' released in 1938 made her a national star.

Ella became a legend making thousands of songs her own. Despite no formal voice training she had the three octave range of an opera star. She combined flawless technique with the spontaneous improvisation of jazz, scat singing becoming her trademark.

Between 1956 and 1964 Ella recorded her crowning achievement, a series of albums each dedicated to the songs of an American composer. Ira Gershwin said: 'I didn't realise our songs were so good until Ella sang them.'

Ella was a tireless performer touring between 40 and 45 weeks of every year. In a remarkable lifetime of song which she sustained until four years before her death, she recorded over 2,000 numbers, sold over 40 million albums and won 13 Grammy Awards.

Left Ella's own experience on Cunarders was very different from the lyrics of her number, 'Ship Without a Sail'.

'Still alone, still at sea Still there's no one to care for me.'

CLARK GABLE
(1901-1960)

King of Hollywood

As a young man Clark Gable was so determined to be an actor that he was prepared to work unpaid. He met and briefly married an acting teacher who arranged to have his teeth fixed and schooled him for stardom.

His first film appearance was in a 1931 Western, 'The Painted Desert'. In 1934 he was propelled to superstardom in the romantic comedy 'It Happened One Night' which held the record for the greatest number of Oscars for forty years. A string of box-office successes followed including six with blonde bombshell, Jean Harlow. He is best remembered today as Rhett Butler in 'Gone With the Wind' (1939), a role which he initially turned down as too demanding.

He found personal happiness with the third of his five wives, the actress Carole Lombard, who tragically died in an air crash in 1942. He then enlisted as a private in the US Army Air Corps. Clark Gable was the favourite film star of Adolf Hitler who issued the order to capture him alive.

Clark Gable became the most highly paid non-studio actor of the 1950s. He died suddenly a fortnight after completing 'The Misfits', co-starring Marilyn Monroe, the stress proving too much for his heart.

Right Stand to attention -
Clark Gable's on board.

PAULETTE GODDARD
(1911-1990)

I do ... I do ... I do ...

Paulette Goddard had a winning way with men. The child model and Ziegfeld Follies Girl married a millionaire when she was only sixteen. She arrived in Hollywood a few years later with $500,000 of alimony in her bank account.

While in the Busby Berkeley chorus line, she caught the eye of Charlie Chaplin who featured her in 'Modern Times' (1936) and 'The Great Dictator' (1940). Their unconventional wedding ceremony at sea in 1936, however, may have cost her the role as Scarlett O'Hara in 'Gone with the Wind' as the producer was concerned about the public's reaction to a star who might not be legally married.

While filming 'Second Chorus' (1940) she danced with Fred Astaire and acted opposite her next husband-to-be, Burgess Meredith who produced and starred with his wife in 'The Diary of a Chambermaid' (1946) in which Paulette gave one of her best performances.

In the 1950s a series of B movies effectively ended her 40-strong film career and she retired to Europe with her last husband, Erich Maria Remarque, the author of one of the great anti-war novels. 'All Quiet on the Western Front'. A wealthy and independent minded woman, in her last years she was a major benefactor of the New York University Tisch School of the Arts.

Left Paulette Goddard and third husband Burgess Meredith wrapped against the chill of New York on the Sports Deck.

SAM GOLDWYN

(1879-1974)

Gelbfisz ... Goldfish ... Goldwyn

Born in Poland, Samuel Gelbfisz emigrated to Britain by walking through Europe. Once Samuel Goldfish had earned enough for his passage, he sailed to Nova Scotia and then walked to New York where he rose from factory sweeper to successful salesman in five years.

His personal obsession was films and in 1913 he formed the Jesse L. Lasky Feature Photoplay Company, hiring unknown writer, Cecil B. DeMille, to direct the first feature 'The Squaw Man' (1914). Although success soon led to a merger Samuel fell out with his partners and with the studio's star, Mary Pickford. The company went on to become Paramount Pictures.

Samuel's next venture was Goldwyn Pictures with Edgar Selwyn: he liked the name so much that he adopted it as his own in 1918. Lone wolf Samuel soon sold out, after again falling out with investors and partners but his name still remains the G in MGM.

Samuel Goldwyn never produced a B movie. He became Hollywood's greatest independent producer releasing films like 'The Best Years of Our Lives' (1946) and 'Guys and Dolls' (1955) over his forty year career. He laid down the model that successful independents have followed ever since - a small unit working on one top quality film at a time with the best writers, actors, producer and director.

Right Busman's holiday! Sam Goldwyn could not resist star spotting even during an ocean voyage.

CARY GRANT
(1904-1986)

'The eighth wonder of the world'

The eighth wonder of the world was how film star Cary Grant described his favourite liner the Queen Mary. He regularly timed his trips across the Atlantic to fit in with her sailing schedule. He met Betsy Drake, one of his five wives, when crossing on the Queen Mary in 1947.

After an unhappy childhood in England, Archibald Alexander Leach joined a travelling acrobatic troupe. During the 1920s he toured England and the USA in vaudeville and theatre. In 1932, newly christened Cary Grant, he made his film debut in 'This is the Night', followed by a string of unremarkable films.

His fortunes changed in 1937 with the end of his studio contract and the freedom to choose his own films. His dashing looks and deadpan delivery rapidly made him a comic leading man starring alongside actresses like Katherine Hepburn, Rosalind Russell and Rita Hayworth. Four films directed by Alfred Hitchcock made him a master of suspense.

In 1962 he turned down the chance to take on a third persona as the suave man of action when he rejected a part in the first James Bond film.

Left Cary Grant in the first-class dining-room on the Queen Mary with Binnie Barnes, the wife of the head of Columbia Pictures and a popular socialite, and her daughter.

REX HARRISON
(1908-1990)

'Sexy Rexy'

Rex Harrison was the ultimate debonair man about town, summed up in his Oscar winning role as Professor Higgins in 'My Fair Lady' (1964).

He began his 50 year stage career in London's West End in the 1930s when, in his view, the theatre was dominated by 'tail-coat actors, who used to wander about the stage as if it were their dressing room.' His skill in black-tie comedy was proven in Terence Rattigan's 'French Without Tears' and Noel Coward's 'Design for Living'. Coward, who later turned down the role of Professor Higgins, described Harrison as 'the best light comedian in the world - after me.'

Following war service in the RAF and a flirtation with Hollywood, Harrison returned to Broadway and the West End. From 1956 he talked his way through the songs of 'My Fair Lady' on stage and then on the wide screen.

In 1963 he played Cleopatra's lover Julius Caesar in the film that made Elizabeth Taylor a legend and four years later charmed a generation of children as 'Dr Doolittle'. Thereafter he largely returned to his first love, the stage, performing until a month before his death. In private life too, he broke women's hearts resulting in six marriages and the affairs that gained him the nickname of 'Sexy Rexy'.

Right Spotted them! Admiring passengers making way for two future Knights of the stage: Rex Harrison seen here on the Queen Mary with his hand over the shoulder of John Mills.

DORIS HART
(1925-)

Game, set and match

Doris Hart did not look set to be a tennis legend. She started playing in Florida as therapy for a knee infection, having had her first encounter with the game through watching people playing outside the window of her hospital ward.

By the age of 16 she was ranked among the top ten players in the world. In 1947 she won the women's doubles at Wimbledon, capping it with her first grand slam singles title in the Australian championships two years later.

Her greatest triumph came at Wimbledon in 1951. Achieving the triple - singles, doubles and mixed - while losing only one set, made her the world's top female tennis player. From 1946-55 she won all 14 of her singles matches and eight out of nine doubles in the Wightman Cup, the annual tennis competition between Britain and the USA. She retired in the mid 1950s to become a coach and write her autobiography 'Tennis With Hart'.

Doris Hart and Australian Margaret Court are the only players in tennis history to win all 12 of the world's major titles at least once.

Left Doris Hart substituting a handbag for a racquet during a welcome home to New York.

RITA HAYWORTH
(1918-1985)

'Love goddess'

Rita Hayworth learned to dance as soon as she could walk. The
Hollywood dream came true when a film executive spotted her dancing
in a nightclub and offered her a screen test. She must have felt at home
in her debut 'Dante's Inferno' (1935) where her dance routine is cut
short by a fire on a gambling ship - she once was a dancer on such a ship
off Mexico.

Columbia Pictures groomed the shy young dancer for stardom. Her
performance as a red headed temptress in 'Blood and Sand' (1941) made
her hot Hollywood property and a wartime GI pin-up girl.

In 1946 she starred in 'Gilda', the film that made her a world sex goddess:
'Every man I have known has fallen in love with Gilda and wakened with
me.' The five husbands who briefly shared her bed included actor/director
Orson Welles and international playboy Prince Aly Khan.

Her last and saddest role was to make her fans aware of a new
disease, Alzheimer's.

Right Although the 'best
dressed girl in Hollywood'
liked to relax during
transatlantic crossings in
sweater and slacks Rita
always looked smart for
the cameramen on the
Queen Elizabeth.

ALFRED HITCHCOCK
(1899-1980)

Hitching a lift

The film career of Alfred Hitchcock started when he approached a new studio in London with an idea for title cards. They liked his work and by 1923 his name appeared for the first time on the credits as an art director.

In 1926 he made his first suspense thriller 'The Lodger' about a man mistaken for Jack the Ripper. By the early 1930s he had not only mastered sound but the cinematic techniques that he was to make his own in films like 'The Thirty-Nine Steps' (1935) and 'The Lady Vanishes' (1938).

Hitchcock was finally lured to Hollywood in 1939 supposedly to work on 'Titanic' which was scrapped being replaced by 'Rebecca' which he helped to win Best Picture of the Year (1940). After propaganda films during the War came some of his greatest nail-biters including 'Notorious' (1946), 'Rear Window' (1955), 'North by Northwest' (1959) and his horror tours de force, 'Psycho' (1960) and 'The Birds' (1963).

Hitchcock said he never read the reviews of the 53 films and 350 TV shows which this shy and modest maestro made simply to please himself and his audience. He claimed that what scared him most were small children, policemen, high places and that his latest picture would not be as good as his last.

Left Alfred Hitchcock making a mysterious exit on the Queen Mary.

BOB HOPE
(1903-2003)

GI Bob

Bob Hope was a natural entertainer even at school: 'He'll tell you three jokes before you say hello.'

In the 1930s he swapped vaudeville for Broadway and Hollywood where he was one of the top ten box office stars for the next two decades. He successfully switched from radio to television co-starring with Lucille Ball in the 1950s sitcom, 'I Love Lucy'.

Bob Hope's quick wit and immensely likeable personality ensured his lasting popularity whether hosting the Oscars, playing golf with US Presidents, entertaining the troops or on 'The Road to…' with Bing Crosby. His Christmas shows were an unforgettable experience for generations of GIs.

Bob's lifelong passion was golf. 'I tell jokes to claim my green fees.' He helped to popularise the game and raised millions of dollars for charity as player and sponsor. He regularly practised his golf drives from the upper decks of the Queen Mary and the QE2.

Bob entered the Guinness Book of Records as the world's most honoured entertainer 'for his contribution to the laughter of the world'.

Right Hope (centre) surrounded by fellow Hollywood stars (left to right) Robert Montgomery, Loretta Young, Alexis Smith and her husband Craig Stevens, on the boat deck of the Queen Mary at Southampton, 1947.

BETTY HUTTON
(1921-)

'The Blonde Bombshell'

As a child Betty Hutton sang for her supper to help support her family after the death of her father. In her teens on her way to Broadway stardom she sang with several bands, her sheer energy earning her the title of 'The Blonde Bombshell' and a billing as 'America's No. 1 Jitterbug'.

She was a natural wartime pin-up from the day she first bounced on to the screen in 'The Fleet's In' (1942). She made a string of musical comedies and biopics over the next decade including 'Annie Get Your Gun' (1950) and a star role as a high-wire artist in Cecil B. DeMille's 'The Greatest Show on Earth' (1952).

The same year she signed her own fate when she walked out on her contract after demanding that her second husband, choreographer Charles O'Curran, direct her films. She only made one more screen appearance, picking up occasional work on Broadway and the night club circuit. Her life changed direction dramatically in 1972 when a Rhode Island priest befriended her after a suicide attempt. She graduated from college and ended her career teaching acting to a new generation of hopefuls, making a final comeback in a stage revival of 'Annie Get Your Gun'.

Right 'The Incendiary Blonde' bewitching her dinner companion at sea.

BUSTER KEATON
(1895-1966)

Caught in the act

Buster was one of film's greatest comics.

He learned his amazing falls and stunts and how to keep a straight face when working as a child in his family's vaudeville troupe. Deadpan got more laughs and also hid the pain.

In 1917 a meeting with vaudeville friend and movie producer Fatty Arbuckle took him into films. His antics as the man who survives against all odds were so successful that he was soon producing films in his own studio. His favourite film 'Our Hospitality' was a family affair with guest appearances by his father and young son. In one of the great stunts of all time Buster rescued his first wife from going over the edge of a waterfall.

The 1930s were difficult years. Two divorces, the loss of control over his productions and a string of low budget films led to drink problems and a mental breakdown. Buster, however, was a survivor writing gags for Clark Gable and the Marx Brothers, forming a double act with his third wife, dancer Eleanor Morris and making guest appearances on film and television at a time when a new generation was discovering and preserving the reels of his silent comedies.

Left The master-at-arms, the Queen Mary's policeman 'apprehends' Buster while Keaton's wife looks on.

HELEN KELLER

(1880-1968)

'Not born to die'

Helen Keller was one of the most remarkable women of the
20th century.

A fever left the toddler from a small town in Alabama deaf and blind.
She coped by clinging to her mother's skirt and making up signs to 'talk'
to her family. If she wanted ice cream, she would hug her shoulders
and shiver.

When seven year old Helen threw temper tantrums in frustration at
her limitations, her parents hired a tutor, Anne Sullivan, who herself
had temporarily lost her sight. Anne understood what Helen Keller's
world was like. She taught her to read, write and speak, helped by
Helen's remarkable memory and her ability to work out what someone
was saying by putting her fingers to their lips. Her teacher remained at
Helen's side for fifty years.

Helen's first book 'The Story of My Life' was translated into 50 languages
and she visited 35 countries to fundraise and encourage society to adopt
a more sympathetic understanding of the blind and the deaf.

Tragically she never saw or heard the two Oscar winning films made
about her life. At her funeral Senator Lister Hill summed up her legacy:
'She will live on, one of the few, the immortal names not born to die'.

Right Helen Keller
(left) 'chatting' with her
travelling companions
in her suite on the
Queen Mary.

KING FAISAL OF IRAQ
(1935-1958)

The Last King

King Faisal II of Iraq was only four when his father died mysteriously after his car crashed into a lamp post. Until his Coronation in 1953, the shy young man was brought up away from the public eye, his uncle assuming the regency. He received an English public school education at Harrow along with his cousin King Hussein of Jordan with whom he became close friends.

When Syria joined with Egypt to form the United Arab Republic, in 1958 the two young rulers responded by creating the Arab Federation of Iraq and Jordan with Faisal at its head. Faisal's short reign ended in the bloody massacre of al-Zuhoor palace on 14th July, 1958 when the Iraqi army marched into Baghdad and proclaimed a republic. Although he was promised safe conduct into exile, the army executed the King and his family.

Right Two young rulers (Faisal, right) who had adopted a Western lifestyle.

BURT LANCASTER
(1913-1994)

A seriously tough guy

This New York streetkid loved turning cartwheels and joined the circus as an acrobat. Introduced to acting in the army during the Second World War he starred on Broadway before heading for Hollywood which he once described as 'nothing more than a big circus'.

The passionate, self taught actor learned the business as he went along, leading the French actress Jeanne Moreau to complain: 'Before he can pick up an ashtray, he has to discuss his motivation for a couple of hours.' His private life was as complex as his on-screen presence.

Left Burt Lancaster (right) enjoying a chat with friend and fellow actor Nick Cravat in the Queen Elizabeth's smoking room.

Initially cast as a tough guy Burt Lancaster's natural dramatic abilities came to the fore in films like 'From Here to Eternity' (1953), 'Birdman of Alcatraz' (1962) and 'Elmer Gantry' (1960) for which he won an Oscar. He financed his love of artistic challenges like Visconti's 'The Leopard' (1963) by signing up for box office hits. One of his strangest roles was reading the alphabet for the children's television series 'Sesame Street'.

STAN LAUREL
& OLIVER HARDY
(1890-1965 & 1892-1957)

'I'm Mr Hardy and this is my friend, Mr Laurel'

The childhood stars first met on a film set. In 1926 when a director wanted to team skinny Stan with a comic 'fat guy' the 25 year partnership of Laurel and Hardy was born.

Stan, the ideas man and gag writer, took on the role of the thin guy with a brain to match who scratched his head if in doubt and burst into tears when in trouble. Ollie was his foil - dignified, blustering impatient, who saw most of his troubles as the result of Stan having got them into 'another fine mess'.

In a lifetime partnership they appeared in over 100 films. Their private lives were more turbulent. Stan had four wives and Oliver, three.

Talkies simply added the new dimension of sound to their quirky relationship. When Oliver suffered a stroke in 1950 Stan returned to writing comedy. A decade later he was awarded a special Oscar for pioneering comedy on film.

Right Stan (right) and Oliver (left) were regular Cunard passengers seen here in a rare picture with their wives.

VERA LYNN

(1917-)

'We'll meet again'

Vera was the forces' sweetheart during the Second World War.

The seven year old launched her singing career by touring working men's clubs in London. She sang with the leading big bands of the 1930s where she met her future husband and manager, saxophonist Harry Lewis.

In 1940 she launched her own BBC radio series 'Sincerely Yours'. She became the link between the girls back home and their men overseas, reading their personal messages over the air and singing sentimental favourites such as 'We'll Meet Again' and 'The White Cliffs of Dover'. She was so popular that one comedian quipped: 'The war was started by Vera Lynn's agent!' Films and personal tours to overseas bases further bolstered her contribution to the war effort.

After the War Vera resumed her radio series and gave variety performances. In 1962 her voice was used to evoke memories of the war years in the West End musical 'Blitz'.

Although she increasingly withdrew from public life Vera could still be persuaded to take people down memory lane. She sang during the celebrations marking the 50th anniversary of D-Day joining the vets as the QE2 sailed past the Normandy beaches.

Left Vera Lynn matching the elegance of the first class dining room on the Queen Elizabeth.

SOMERSET MAUGHAM
(1874-1965)

A short story . . . a long life

W. Somerset Maugham was one of the 20th century's most prolific and popular writers.

Born in the British Embassy in Paris, he trained as a surgeon until his first novel 'Liza of Lambeth', based on his experiences as a young doctor in the London slums, proved a bestseller. He turned to writing full-time and by 1908 four of his plays were running simultaneously in the West End.

During the First World War Maugham served with the Red Cross in France, where he fell in love with a young American Gerald Haxton, and as a secret agent in Geneva and St Petersburg. Although Maugham married Syrie Wellcome, after her drugs millionaire husband divorced her, he remained Haxton's lover for the next forty years. In his semi-autobiographical novel 'Of Human Bondage' (1915), Maugham wrote movingly of sexual obsession and freedom.

Although today he is best remembered as the master of the modern short story, in the 1920s Maugham wrote a series of plays, the royalties from which made him a very wealthy man. In 1929 he bought a house on the French Riviera where he attracted a colony of writers and artists and where the guest list read like a Who's Who from Winston Churchill to the Windsors.

Right On an ocean liner Somerset Maugham found plenty of material for his next short story.

UP TO BOAT DECK
     SUN DECK
SQUASH RACKET CO
     GYMNASIUM
     SPORTS DECK

RAY MILLAND
(1907-1986)

Dial 54 for Marriage

Born Reginald Alfred Truscott-Jones, his agent insisted that the young Welsh member of the Royal Household Cavalry must change his name if he wanted a career in films. Ray Milland set off for Hollywood in 1930.

Charming, debonair and self-assured, he was typecast as the romantic lead in light drawing room comedies until his performance as an alcoholic writer in 'The Lost Weekend' won him critical acclaim and an Oscar in 1945. Nine years later he played opposite Grace Kelly as the suave tennis star who plans to murder his wife in Alfred Hitchcock's suspense classic 'Dial M For Murder'.

Thereafter his career somewhat faltered although he had a successful comedy show on TV and directed himself in a number of films. After a cameo role in the ultimate tear-jerker 'Love Story' (1970) he turned increasingly to low- budget horror movies like 'The Thing With Two Heads' where the other half of the monster was former footballer Rosie Grier.

Left No time even to take off her hat - Ray Milland and his wife on leaving New York.

Off-screen Milland was of little interest to the gossip columnists and shunned the glitz of Hollywood. He was an intensely private man who loved books, his home and his wife to whom he was married for 54 years.

VISCOUNT MONTGOMERY
(1887-1976)

Warlord extraordinaire

Monty was one of the most inspirational leaders of the Second World War.

On leaving school he joined the British army, serving as a young officer on the front during the First World War. In 1939 he commanded part of the British Expeditionary Force which had to be evacuated from Dunkirk. In 1943 he was the hero of the Battle of El Alamein, the first significant German defeat of the Second World War.

The non-smoking, teetotal soldier led a simple life, choosing to live in a caravan in the garden of the luxurious house assigned to him during the North African campaign. He was popular with the ranks, believing that an officer's first battle was to win the hearts of his men.

He led the British and Canadian troops at the D-Day landings and, promoted to Field Marshal in September 1944, was the senior British military commander in the west European war zone. On 4th May, 1945 he accepted the formal German surrender.

From 1951-1958 he was Deputy Supreme Commander of NATO forces in Europe under General Eisenhower, travelling on the Queen Mary for his frequent trips to the States.

Right Monty enjoying the company of film actresses Bonita Granville and Janis Page on the Queen Mary.

ANNA NEAGLE
(1904-1986)

Aristocrat, heroine and Queen

Londoner Anna Neagle was a chorus girl and aspiring actress until discovered by film director Herbert Wilcox who shaped her career and became her husband in 1943.

Each decade was associated with a different type of role. In the 1930s she played royalty moving on from bouncing mistress in 'Nell Gwyn' (1934) to stately monarch in 'Victoria the Great' (1937) and its sequel 'Sixty Glorious Years' (1938). In the 1940s she turned to strong-minded women from pioneer of flight Amy Johnson to nurse Edith Cavell and Resistance heroine Odette. From the late 1940s she featured in the upper class dramas and romantic musicals like 'The Courtneys of Curzon Street' (1947) which collectively became known as the 'Mayfair cycle'.

Although she briefly crossed the Atlantic to Hollywood she failed to gain the same popularity with an American public as she had won in Britain where she was voted the top British female star in seven consecutive years. She also made it to the Guinness Book of Records for her 2,062 performances in the stage musical 'Charlie Girl' from 1965 to 1971, two years after she was made a Dame of the British Empire for her services to acting. She was still onstage only a few weeks before her death.

Left Anna with an admirer's bouquet in her stateroom on the Queen Mary.

DAVID NIVEN
(1910-1983)

Around the world in eighty days

Training as a British Army officer stood David Niven in good stead when he decided to hang up his boots and try his luck in Hollywood. His charm and good breeding won him an entrée to the smart set led by film stars Clark Gable and Errol Flynn. His military background made him a natural to cast in films like 'The Charge of the Light Brigade' (1936), 'The Prisoner of Zenda' (1937) and 'The Dawn Patrol' (1938).

Colonel David Niven returned to real life action during the Second World War although he was granted leave to appear in the morale boosting films 'The First of the Few' (1942) and 'The Way Ahead' (1944). He spent the next 30 years in constant demand on both sides of the Atlantic as the dashing, debonair leading man, being perfectly cast as the gentleman voyager Phileas Fogg in 'Around the World in 80 Days' (1956). He won an Oscar for his role as a disgraced military officer in 'Separate Tables' (1958).

Witty, loyal to his many friends and an inimitable raconteur, David Niven regularly kept passengers on the Queen Mary enthralled with stories of his colourful life.

Right Table for two for David and his second wife Swedish model Hjordis Tersmeden.

IVOR NOVELLO
(1893-1951)

On the crest of the wave

It was while Welshman David Ivor Davies was a chorister at the Magdalen College Choir School in Oxford that he started composing under the name, Ivor Novello. In 1915 he set to music 'Keep the Home Fires Burning', the song that made him a legend overnight. Countless troops sang it as they waved farewell to their families on their way to the trenches during the First World War.

Following a wartime career as a pilot where he survived two crash landings, Novello made his film debut in the romantic drama 'Call of the Blood' (1919). A classic matinée idol, Novello went on to make another 15 silent films before transferring to the talkies. He decided, however, to return to his first loves - the stage and composing music.

Over the next two decades he wrote eight frothy, romantic musicals including 'Glamorous Night', 'Crest of the Wave' and 'The Dancing Years' (1939), performing in six of them himself as lead actor. Women queued at the stage door for a glimpse of their dark haired idol.

On 6th March 1951, Novello died in his flat above the Strand Theatre just four hours after performing the lead in his own production, 'King's Rhapsody'. His legacy to the world was over 250 songs with titles like 'Deep in My Heart' and 'Shine Through My Dreams'.

Left Ivor Novello (far right) with a troupe of friends on the Queen Elizabeth.

MARGARET O'BRIEN
(1937-)

Hollywood babe

Margaret O'Brien has been described as the 'greatest little actress of all time'. Her face was more familiar to 1940s cinemagoers than that of many adult stars, the quality of her acting setting her apart from other 'cute kids' of her day.

When Hollywood spotted her face on a magazine cover, the four year old was offered a one minute spot in 'Babes on Broadway' (1941): Her first lines were 'Please! Please! Don't send my brother to the chair! Don't let him burn!' Audiences took her to their hearts in her second role as an orphan in wartime London.

Hailed as the new Shirley Temple, Margaret's film studio set about finding appropriate parts to display her prodigious talent. They devised vehicles like a recitation of Abraham Lincoln's Gettysburg Address to keep her in the public eye as well as boosting wartime morale. She was awarded a special Oscar for her performance as Tootie, Judy Garland's youngest sister in the musical 'Meet Me in St Louis' (1944).

With a lessening demand for 'feel good movies' after the War, Margaret started to experience growing pains, although a series of heart rending dramas kept her face on the screen including two 1949 film adaptations of children's novels - 'Little Women' and 'The Secret Garden'. She failed to make the difficult transition into adult roles, building a new life in television and charity work.

Right Every ship has a cat. Margaret O'Brien showing hers round her stateroom.

JACQUELINE ONASSIS
(1929-1994)

'All the money in the world'

Jacqueline Lee Bouvier enjoyed a privileged childhood being crowned Debutante of the Year in 1948. While working as a newspaper photographer in Washington DC she met the capital's most eligible bachelor and the man who was to put her photograph on the front pages - Senator John F. Kennedy.

His inauguration as President of the United States in 1961 brought a beautiful young wife and the first young children for half a century to the White House. Jackie added charm, intelligence and culture to the role of First Lady while her priority remained 'to take care of the President'.

Jackie's courageous dignity after Kennedy's assassination in 1963 won her the world's admiration. In 1968 the tragedy was re-enacted when Bobby, the President's brother and Jackie's closest friend, was shot. Shortly thereafter she married Aristotle Onassis, Greek shipping magnate, international jetsetter and one of the world's richest men. He once admitted that 'If women didn't exist, all the money in the world would have no meaning'.

Onassis offered her respite from the Kennedy legend and the privacy of a Greek island on which to bring up her children. Widowed again in 1975 she retired from the public eye as an editor for a New York publisher.

Left The Kennedy clan in their Cunard cabin.

ELEANOR PARKER
(1922-)

'The woman of a thousand faces'

The ravishing red head already had already some acting experience under her belt when Warner Brothers signed her on her 19th birthday.

She cut her teeth on B movies before starring in 'Pride of the Marines' (1945). Two years later her leading man was the future President of the USA, Ronald Reagan. She proved a versatile actress, winning three Oscar nominations in the early 1950s for roles as different as a terrorised prison inmate, a neglected wife with a secret and an opera star struck down by polio. Her adaptability was such that audiences never knew in advance what her next role would be.

Her leading men read like a Who's Who of Hollywood - Humphrey Bogart, Kirk Douglas, Errol Flynn, Clark Gable, Charlton Heston, Robert Mitchum and Frank Sinatra. In real life she fell in love and married four times.

Although her career peaked by the 1960s she continued to appear in support roles including the baroness in 'The Sound of Music' (1965) and in television dramas before retiring to Palm Springs.

Right Eleanor Parker posing for the camera as the Queen Elizabeth steams up the Hudson River.

FRED PERRY
(1909-1995)

Anyone for tennis . . .

To this day Fred Perry remains unbeaten champion of British tennis.

Lawn tennis was his second love, having won the world table tennis championship in 1929.

Mastery of his powerful forehand stroke launched him on his way to three Wimbledon singles victories and three US Championships. His physique was perfect for the game while his breezy self-confidence and cheeky grin won the hearts of the crowd.

In 1933 he led the team that brought the Davis Cup back to Britain from France after 21 years. Perry and fellow player 'Bunny' Austin were carried shoulder high by the crowds when they arrived at Victoria Station on their return from Paris. Bunny, who had met his wife on a Cunarder four years earlier, was the inventor of tennis shorts: at the time men played in heavy, sweat soaked cricket flannels.

Until Fred Perry, Britain had not produced a Wimbledon singles champion for quarter of a century. It has yet to produce another winner.

Right Fred Perry taking a break on the deck stairs.

SIR MICHAEL REDGRAVE
(1908-1985)

Knight of the theatre

In 1934 school teacher Michael Redgrave became an actor, first appearing at the Liverpool Playhouse where he met and married his wife. He then joined Sir John Gielgud's famous Old Vic theatre company in London.

Redgrave was never entirely comfortable with the cinema claiming that he found film acting suspiciously easy and that he only took the lead in Hitchcock's 'The Lady Vanishes' (1938) because he had a family to support. He also played a miner's son in 'The Stars Look Down' (1939) and Barnes Wallis, the inventor of the bouncing bomb, in 'The Dam Busters' (1955). He was nominated for an Oscar for his part in 'Mourning Becomes Electra' (1947).

He is best remembered as a classical Shakespearean actor, enthralling audiences with his interpretation of Richard II, Prospero, King Lear, Antony, Shylock and Hamlet. During the mid 1970s he introduced Shakespeare to worldwide audiences with touring productions like 'The Hollow Crown'.

Left Rather than reliving the balcony scene from Romeo and Juliet Sir Michael is in fact heading for a spot of fresh air on the sports deck.

No longer able to learn lines due to the onset of Parkinson's disease, in 1979 he gave his final performance in 'Close of Play' where although he had only one line he was required to remain on stage throughout. Himself the son of a silent film star, Sir Michael Redgrave and his actress wife Rachel Kempson founded a remarkable theatrical dynasty through their three children - Vanessa, Corin and Lynn.

ELIZABETH TAYLOR
(1932-)

'America's longest reigning glamour queen'

Elizabeth Taylor always wanted to be an actress like her mother. The stunningly beautiful ten year old realised her ambition with her first film role in 'There's One Born Every Minute' (1942). She went on to star in 'Lassie Come Home' (1943), 'National Velvet' (1944) and 'Little Women' (1949).

She moved effortlessly into adult roles. 'The most beautiful woman in the world' broke all records by commanding a fee of one million dollars to star as 'Cleopatra' (1963). She won two Oscars as a disillusioned call girl in 'Butterfield 8' (1960) and as a middle-aged tigress battling it out with her real-life husband Richard Burton in 'Who's Afraid of Virginia Woolf' (1966).

Elizabeth Taylor became as famous for her eight marriages as for her screen roles. Cunarders provided the backdrop for some of the drama. In 1950 she honeymooned with hotel chain heir Nicky Hilton on the Queen Elizabeth, her new husband surprising passengers by playing cards in the smoking room until the small hours. She regularly travelled Cunard with her producer husband Mike Todd before his death in an air crash and partied all night with the actor Richard Burton whom she married twice.

Left A young Elizabeth Taylor on the sports deck of the Queen Mary where she regularly exercised her pampered pets. She ordered special meals for them from the fish chef.

SPENCER TRACY
(1900-1967)

No matinée idol

Spencer Tracy sought adventure from his earliest days. After being expelled from 15 schools, serving in the navy and a spell at college, he made his stage debut as a robot. By the end of the 1920s he had won a reputation as a solid, workmanlike actor.

His big break came in 1930 when he played 'Killer' Mears in a tough prison drama on Broadway leading to a Hollywood role in a comedy about prison life. For the next few years he was typecast as gangster, racketeer and tough guy, his wider acting talents only being recognised from 1935 when he moved to MGM for whom he was to make over 30 pictures. His craggy face, versatility and seemingly effortless understated style earned him more Academy Award nominations than any other actor of his era as well as Oscars in 'Captains Courageous' (1937) and 'Boys' Town' (1938).

Although Tracy had a reputation as a hard drinking womaniser who took up with his leading ladies, he put aside his wild ways on meeting Katherine Hepburn on the set of 'Woman of the Year' (1942), the start of a romantic and professional partnership that lasted the rest of his life. Only weeks before his death they completed their last film together, the comedy 'Guess Who's Coming to Dinner' (1967).

Right Spencer Tracy (right) and fellow film star Charles Boyer deep in conversation as they put their feet up on deck.

JOHNNY WEISMULLER
(1904-1984)

Me Tarzan . . . you Jane

In 1921 the Romanian born swimmer lost his first and only official race thanks to trouble with his bathing cap. Soon sports journalists were calling him 'Prince of the Waves', 'the Human Hydroplane' and 'the Chicago Whirlwind' as he broke world records.

Retiring in 1929 after picking up five Olympic golds, Johnny went on the road giving swimming exhibitions and promoting swimwear until a dip in the Hollywood Athletic Club pool changed his career again. He was spotted by a screenwriter who was working on a new film based on Tarzan, the Lord of the Jungle.

'Tarzan, the Ape Man' (1932) made Johnny an overnight sensation. Dialogue was kept to a minimum because of his high pitched voice and difficulty in learning lines. His wild personal life and a series of Tarzan films with Maureen O'Sullivan as Jane kept Johnny in the news.

During the Second World War Johnny raised millions of dollars, the GIs requesting his Tarzan yell to be broadcast on the battle front. In 1948 Johnny took on a new role as Jungle Jim. Five marriages and a Hollywood lifestyle, however, took their financial toll and by the early 1970s he was a greeter at Caesar's Palace, Las Vegas.

Right Johnny knew the ropes on the Queen Mary. One passenger recalled: 'he came down in his trunks and it's in the winter of course and the ship's rolling. He dived off the balcony and to all of us kids – that's Tarzan. We jumped on him and he's throwing us all over the place.'

H.G. WELLS
(1866-1946)

The man who tried to invent the future

H. G. Wells was a literary giant of the early 20th century: a master of comedy, a pioneer of science fiction and a prophet of the shape of things to come.

Studying science at London University fired the imagination of the shopkeeper's son. By his early thirties he had published 'The Invisible Man', 'The Time Machine' and 'The War of the Worlds'. In the 1900s he turned to comic fiction, creating everyday heroes that ordinary people could identify with like Mr Kipps and Mr Polly.

In five decades as an author Wells wrote over 100 books. Both through his fiction and his popular scientific writings he showed a remarkable vision, foretelling the atom bomb, the fourth dimension of time, 'designer creatures' and a 'world brain' not unlike the Internet.

Wells' private life was stormy. As a believer in free love he practised what he preached. He had two wives and many lovers, fathering several illegitimate children. The great Irish playwright, George Bernard Shaw, said of him: 'The worse he behaved, the more he was indulged and the more he was indulged, the worse he behaved.'

Left Immensely popular on both sides of the Atlantic H. G. Wells browses the books and magazines on the Queen Mary.

MAE WEST
(1893-1980)

Come up and see me

After playing Little Nell in a long running melodrama, New Yorker Mae West joined a vaudeville company where, aged 16 she married her song and dance partner, a secret she kept from her fans for over thirty years.

She quickly became a Broadway star and one of vaudeville's few solo female performers, famous for her tight fitting dresses, enormous plumed hats, provocative remarks and throaty singing voice. In 1926 she wrote a play entitled 'Sex' which resulted in the cast being arrested during its 41st week and Mae serving ten days in prison for 'corrupting the morals of youth'. Her third play contained her immortal line - 'Why don't you come up and see me sometime?' - addressed to a Salvation Army captain.

When two later plays were censored, she moved to Hollywood in the early 1930s hoping to find greater artistic freedom. Based on one of her plays, her second film 'She Done Him Wrong' (1933) introduced a young Cary Grant who also partnered her in 'I'm No Angel' (1933). She scripted 'My Little Chickadee' (1940) in which she made a perfect comedy duo with W.C. Fields. When her film career faltered she returned to Broadway, later touring as a nightclub entertainer and making cameo appearances on film.

Right Is it the ventilator or my hat? Mae West struggling with a stiff breeze on board.

TENNESSEE WILLIAMS
(1911-1983)

A liner called desire

American playwright Tennessee Williams had a lonely childhood marked by illness and bullying due to his lack of masculinity: his father called him 'Miss Nancy'. He started writing and drinking as a means of escape. In 1939 a short story caught the eye of a literary agent who promoted his talent as a playwright. His first production, however, was a disaster, closing after two weeks of its pre-New York run.

A brief spell as a script writer with MGM allowed him time to rework a play, drawing on his childhood experiences, which the studio had rejected: 'The Glass Menagerie' (1945) ran for two years on Broadway. Williams drew on his feelings of depression and isolation to write 'A Streetcar Named Desire' (1947) which won him a Pulitzer Prize: he won his second with 'Cat On a Hot Tin Roof' (1955).

'Suddenly Last Summer' emerged from another period of depression and alcohol dependence in the late 1950s. Although the Gothic tale of repressed sexuality shocked many in the audience, it proved another masterpiece. In 1961 'The Night of the Iguana' won Williams his fourth and final New York Drama Critics Circle Award.

Two years later depression and drugs overwhelmed him after the death of his lover, Frank Marlo. His last play 'Something Cloudy, Something Clear' (1982) was a memorial to their relationship and to William's troubled life.

Left Dining in the first class restaurant on the Queen Mary.

THE DUKE OF WINDSOR
(1894-1972)

Feeling the pinch

The Windsors set the seal on a Cunard Atlantic crossing as the ultimate in chic.

In 1936 the world's most eligible bachelor stunned the world by choosing divorced American socialite, Wallis Simpson, over the British throne.

After his abdication the exiles travelled the world, surrounding themselves with film stars, American millionaires, authors and playwrights. Advance publicity that the Windsors might be sailing Cunard caused tickets for the passage to sell out months in advance. Up to 150 pieces of monogrammed Louis Vuitton luggage marked their arrival on board.

Cunard's staff came to know the Windsors well. The restless Duke liked to watch the bellboys' roll-call at 7am and to join the captain on the bridge late at night where he chatted to the watch and contentedly puffed his pipe. He played endless games of canasta with the Duchess who limited him to one brandy after dinner. The Duchess soon tired of the honour of dining at the captain's table, once declaring that: 'Ships' captains are inclined to pinch.'

After Cunard hinted that the Windsor luggage was becoming excessive, in the 1950s the rival United States Line successfully wooed the couple with the offer of their own main deck suite for the lowest class fare.

Right The Windsors giving one of their pampered pets a sniff of the sea breezes.